My Life and My Thoughts Before and After Moving

The Essential Moving Guided Journal

For Teens

Created By **Sara Elizabeth Boehm**

Sincere thanks to Abby Rollinger for her insights, assistance, and edits, all of which greatly enhanced this journal

Cover Design: Ashley Boehm

Cover quote: "When writing the story of your life, don't let anyone else hold the pen." – Unknown

Second Edition

Introduction

Section One: Before the Move

Section Two: After the Move

Introduction

I'm sure you have heard it said that writing down what you are thinking can help you feel a bit better. Whether what you feel is stress, sadness, anger, or confusion, getting your thoughts out of your head and onto paper can help take away the weight dragging you down and help you process what is going on. This guided journal is designed to help you work through your own journey throughout your move. From before the move to after you have settled in, you can use the prompts in this journal as a general guide to help you write about your experiences from your perspective. If you come to a question that you don't want to write about, cross it out and create your own! Journal here or use these prompts to fill your own online journal or blog, document your move through pictures, write stories, or jot down short thoughts throughout the day. The format doesn't matter, simply do what best fits your style.

And remember that you are not alone. Talk to others who have moved and can relate to what you are going through. Read books on teens moving with their families or search online hashtags like #moving and #newkidintown to see others who are on their own moving journeys.

Ultimately, a move is a uniquely personal experience, and how you process it is absolutely up to you. That being said, there are certain things that you can do and consider that may help ease some of the pain that often comes with a move. But it is up to you: to process, to explore, to take chances, and to make your new life what you want it to be while appreciating and never forgetting where you came from!

~Before the Move~

"When one door of happiness closes, another opens; but often we look so long at the closed door that we do not see the one which has been opened for us." – Helen Keller

When I first heard we were moving, I felt . . .
Now, I feel . . .

_____

_____

_____

_____

_____

_____

_____

_____

_____

_____

_____

_____

_____

_____

_____

_____

_____

_____

_____

_____

_____

_____

_____

_____

_____

_____

_____

_____

_____

_____

_____

_____

_____

_____

_____

_____

"When things are bad, we take comfort in the thought that they could always get worse. And when they are, we find hope in the thought that things are so bad they have to get better." – Malcolm S. Forbes

The hardest part about moving will be . . .

_____

_____

_____

_____

_____

_____

_____

_____

_____

_____

_____

_____

_____

_____

_____

_____

_____

_____

_____

_____

_____

_____

_____

_____

_____

_____

_____

_____

_____

_____

_____

_____

_____

_____

_____

_____

_____

"Sometimes life hits you in the head with a brick. Don't lose faith."
– Steve Jobs

What concerns me most about moving is . . .

_____

_____

_____

_____

_____

_____

_____

_____

_____

_____

_____

_____

_____

_____

_____

_____

_____

_____

_____

"Courage is being scared to death—and saddling up anyway."
– John Wayne

The things I will miss most when I move are . . .

_____

_____

_____

_____

_____

_____

_____

_____

_____

_____

_____

_____

_____

_____

_____

_____

_____

_____

_____

_____

_____

_____

_____

_____

_____

_____

_____

_____

_____

_____

_____

_____

_____

_____

_____

_____

_____

_____

"Time has a wonderful way of showing us what really matters."
– Unknown

The things I will miss least when I move are . . .

_____

_____

_____

_____

_____

_____

_____

_____

_____

_____

_____

_____

_____

_____

_____

_____

_____

_____

_____

_____

_____

"You have brains in your head. You have feet in your shoes. You can steer yourself any direction you choose." – Dr. Seuss

How does the rest of your family feel about the move?
How will the move be challenging for each of them?

_____

_____

_____

_____

_____

_____

_____

_____

_____

_____

_____

_____

_____

_____

_____

_____

_____

_____

_____

_____

_____

_____

_____

_____

_____

_____

_____

_____

_____

_____

_____

_____

_____

_____

_____

_____

_____

"Never forget where you've been, never lose sight of where you are going, and never take for granted the people who travel the journey with you."
– Anonymous

Thinking about the move and my new home and school, I am most excited about . . .

_____

_____

_____

_____

_____

_____

_____

_____

_____

_____

_____

_____

_____

_____

_____

_____

_____

_____

_____

_____

_____

_____

_____

_____

_____

_____

_____

_____

_____

_____

_____

_____

_____

_____

"Incredible change happens in your life when you decide to take control of what you do have power over instead of craving control over what you don't." – Steve Maraboli

I feel lucky that . . .

_____

_____

_____

_____

_____

_____

_____

_____

_____

_____

_____

_____

_____

_____

_____

_____

_____

_____

_____

_____

_____

_____

_____

_____

_____

_____

_____

_____

_____

_____

_____

_____

_____

_____

_____

_____

_____

_____

_____

_____

_____

_____

"Life is 10% what happens to me and 90% how I react to it." – Charles Swindoll

Is there anything you want to know about the move that you haven't asked? How can you find this information?

_____

_____

_____

_____

_____

_____

_____

_____

_____

_____

_____

_____

_____

_____

_____

_____

_____

_____

_____

_____

_____

_____

_____

_____

_____

_____

_____

_____

_____

_____

_____

_____

_____

_____

_____

_____

_____

_____

_____

"The single biggest problem with communication is the illusion that it has taken place." – George Bernard Shaw

Describe a few of your favorite memories from your time in your current home and school. . .

_____

_____

_____

_____

_____

_____

_____

_____

_____

_____

_____

_____

_____

_____

_____

_____

_____

_____

_____

_____

_____

_____

_____

_____

_____

_____

_____

_____

_____

_____

_____

_____

_____

_____

_____

_____

_____

_____

_____

"No matter what happens. . . some memories can never be replaced."
– Unknown

How did your friends react when you told them you were going to move?

_____

_____

_____

_____

_____

_____

_____

_____

_____

_____

_____

_____

_____

_____

_____

_____

_____

_____

_____

_____

_____

_____

_____

_____

_____

_____

_____

_____

_____

_____

_____

_____

_____

_____

_____

You're not the only one experiencing pain and loss during your move—your friends are, too. You will no longer be there every day in person to eat lunch with at school or to hang out with on the weekends. Understand that they may process this pain in different ways, and know that if you are close enough, your friendship with survive in the long run.

Make a bucket list of some places you want to visit and things you want to do one last time before moving:

_____

_____

_____

_____

_____

_____

_____

_____

_____

_____

_____

_____

_____

_____

_____

_____

_____

_____

"Action may not always bring happiness; but there is no happiness without action." – Benjamin Disraeli

How do you plan to say goodbye to your friends before the move? Who do you want to be sure to see?

_____

_____

_____

_____

_____

_____

_____

_____

_____

_____

_____

_____

_____

_____

_____

_____

_____

_____

_____

_____

_____

_____

_____

_____

_____

_____

_____

_____

_____

_____

_____

_____

_____

_____

_____

_____

Make a list of the people you want to be sure to see before you leave. Consider having a party so you can see everyone at once, or plan one on one time with your best friends. Take pictures or leave one another with a memento to keep you close when you are separated.

How do you plan to stay in touch with your current friends after you move?

_____

_____

_____

_____

_____

_____

_____

_____

_____

_____

_____

_____

_____

_____

_____

_____

_____

_____

_____

_____

_____

_____

_____

_____

_____

_____

_____

_____

_____

_____

_____

_____

_____

_____

_____

_____

_____

_____

_____

_____

_____

"Some people come into our lives and quickly go. Some stay for a while, leave footprints on our hearts, and we are never, ever the same." – Flavia Weedn

What do you do to relax? Have you been doing a good job at making sure you aren't too stressed?

_____

_____

_____

_____

_____

_____

_____

_____

_____

_____

_____

_____

_____

_____

_____

_____

_____

_____

"Tension is who you think you should be. Relaxation is who you are."
– Chinese Proverb

Describe a time in the past when you were new to a situation. How did you handle it? What would you do again? What would you do differently?

_____

_____

_____

_____

_____

_____

_____

_____

_____

_____

_____

_____

_____

_____

_____

_____

_____

_____

_____

_____

_____

_____

_____

_____

_____

_____

_____

_____

_____

_____

_____

_____

_____

_____

_____

_____

_____

_____

"When you focus on problems, you'll have more problems. When you focus on possibilities, you'll have more opportunities." – Unknown

3 things that I am grateful for are . . .

_____

_____

_____

_____

_____

_____

_____

_____

_____

_____

_____

_____

_____

_____

_____

_____

_____

_____

_____

_____

_____

_____

_____

_____

_____

_____

_____

_____

_____

_____

_____

_____

_____

_____

_____

_____

_____

_____

_____

_____

_____

_____

_____

"Never let the things you want make you forget the things you have."
– Anonymous

What is it about you that makes you a good friend?

_____

_____

_____

_____

_____

_____

_____

_____

_____

_____

_____

_____

_____

_____

_____

_____

_____

_____

_____

_____

_____

_____

_____

_____

_____

_____

_____

_____

_____

_____

_____

_____

_____

_____

_____

_____

_____

"I've learned that people will forget what you said, people will forget what
you did, but people will never forget how you made them feel."
– Maya Angelou

What do you look for in a close friend?

_____

_____

_____

_____

_____

_____

_____

_____

_____

_____

_____

_____

_____

_____

_____

_____

_____

_____

_____

_____

_____

_____

_____

_____

_____

_____

_____

_____

_____

_____

_____

_____

_____

_____

_____

_____

_____

_____

"People inspire you, or they drain you. Pick them wisely." – Hans F. Hansen

What activities make you happiest?

_____

_____

_____

_____

_____

_____

_____

_____

_____

_____

_____

_____

_____

_____

_____

_____

_____

_____

_____

"To be yourself in a world that is constantly trying to make you something else is the greatest accomplishment." – Ralph Waldo Emerson

How do you plan to make friends in your new school?

_____

_____

_____

_____

_____

_____

_____

_____

_____

_____

_____

_____

_____

_____

_____

_____

_____

_____

_____

_Smile, be open and friendly, take the initiative to talk to others, and don't be
discouraged- it takes time to develop good friendships, but each day brings you one step
closer._

What are the ways you can make your new room and home feel more comfortable?

_____

_____

_____

_____

_____

_____

_____

_____

_____

_____

_____

_____

_____

_____

_____

_____

_____

_____

_____

_____

_____

_____

_____

_____

_____

_____

_____

_____

_____

_____

_____

_____

_____

_____

_____

Make a goal to unpack your things as quickly as possible so you will be surrounded by familiar belongings. Try to put out pictures and other things that remind you of those who love and support you. Use this fresh start to spring clean or re-arrange/ re-decorate.

What makes you nervous? Can you address any of these concerns by talking to others?

_____

_____

_____

_____

_____

_____

_____

_____

_____

_____

_____

_____

_____

_____

_____

_____

_____

_____

_____

_____

_____

_____

_____

_____

_____

_____

_____

_____

_____

_____

_____

_____

_____

_____

_____

_____

_____

_____

"Be strong enough to stand alone, smart enough to know when you need help, and brave enough to ask for it." – Unknown

Is there anything you need to be sure to do before you leave, such as saying goodbye to a favorite teacher or returning something you've recently borrowed?

_____

_____

_____

_____

_____

_____

_____

_____

_____

_____

_____

_____

_____

_____

_____

_____

"A good plan is like a road map. It shows the final destination and usually marks the best way to get there. . ." – H. Stanley Judd

What groups/clubs/activities are you most looking forward to joining after you move?

_____

_____

_____

_____

_____

_____

_____

_____

_____

_____

_____

_____

_____

_____

_____

_____

_____

_____

_____

_____

_____

_____

_____

_____

_____

_____

_____

_____

_____

_____

_____

_____

_____

_____

_____

_____

_____

"Things turn out best for the people who make the best of the way things turn out." – John Wooden

3 things that made me happy today:

_____

_____

_____

_____

_____

_____

_____

_____

_____

_____

_____

_____

_____

_____

_____

_____

_____

_____

_____

_____

"Everything will be okay in the end. If it's not okay, it's not the end."
– John Lennon

Moving is a fresh start—in what way will you make this move a fresh start for you?

_____

_____

_____

_____

_____

_____

_____

_____

_____

_____

_____

_____

_____

_____

_____

_____

_____

_____

_____

"Every day is a second chance." – Unknown

What do you know about your new school? What would you like to know?

_____

_____

_____

_____

_____

_____

_____

_____

_____

_____

_____

_____

_____

_____

_____

_____

_____

_____

_____

_____

_____

_____

_____

_____

_____

_____

_____

_____

_____

_____

_____

_____

_____

_____

_____

_____

"If you don't like something change it; if you can't change it, change the
way you think about it." – Mary Engelbreit

What do you know about your new house? What would you like to know?

_____

_____

_____

_____

_____

_____

_____

_____

_____

_____

_____

_____

_____

_____

_____

_____

_____

_____

"Every day do something that will inch you closer to a better tomorrow."
– Unknown

How are you getting to your new house? What are your plans to keep yourself entertained during the trip?

_____

_____

_____

_____

_____

_____

_____

_____

_____

_____

_____

_____

_____

_____

_____

_____

"One's destination is never a place, but a new way of seeing things."
– Henry Miller

What are you setting aside and not packing so that you have it with you throughout the move and for your first night in your new home?

_____

_____

_____

_____

_____

_____

_____

_____

_____

_____

_____

_____

_____

_____

_____

_____

Fill a backpack or bag to bring with you during the move. Include items like clothes, pajamas, toiletries, as well as any entertainment you'll want on the trip. Set the bag aside in a safe place during the packing process to ensure that it doesn't get packed away!

What was your favorite memory from the past week?

_____

_____

_____

_____

_____

_____

_____

_____

_____

_____

_____

_____

_____

_____

_____

_____

_____

_____

_____

_____

_____

_____

_____

_____

_____

_____

_____

_____

_____

_____

_____

_____

_____

_____

_____

_____

_____

_____

_____

_____

"The reason we struggle with insecurity is because we compare our behind-the-scenes with everyone else's highlight reel." – Steve Furtick

~~~~~~

Your Move in Pictures:

Take time throughout your move to capture your
experiences in pictures. Share them, look back on them
once you have settled in, and keep them for years to come.

Before you move, capture memories to take with you.
During the move, document your journey. After the move,
snap pics to show your old friends so they can visualize
you in your next chapter of life.

Take pictures of:
- Your current house, yard, and room
- Any favorite places around town
- Your current school
- You with your friends and classmates
- Your house in transition during the packing process
- Your trip to your new home
- Your new house, yard, and room
- Your new school
- Any fun finds and discoveries in your new town

~~~~~~

~After the Move~

"We either make ourselves miserable or we make ourselves strong. The amount of work is the same." – Carlos Castenada

Describe the day of the move. How did it go? How did you feel?

_____

_____

_____

_____

_____

_____

_____

_____

_____

_____

_____

_____

_____

_____

_____

_____

_____

_____

_____

_____

_____

_____

_____

_____

_____

_____

_____

_____

_____

_____

_____

_____

_____

_____

_____

_____

_____

_____

_____

_____

"A good laugh and a long sleep are the two best cures for anything."
– Irish proverb

Describe what "home" means to you . . .

_____

_____

_____

_____

_____

_____

_____

_____

_____

_____

_____

_____

_____

_____

_____

_____

_____

_____

_____

_____

_____

_____

_____

_____

_____

_____

_____

_____

_____

_____

_____

_____

_____

_____

_____

_____

_____

_____

_____

_____

"There's no place like home." – Dorothy, *"The Wizard of Oz"*

3 things that I am grateful for are. . .

_____

_____

_____

_____

_____

_____

_____

_____

_____

_____

_____

_____

_____

_____

_____

_____

_____

_____

_____

_____

_____

_____

_____

_____

_____

_____

_____

_____

_____

_____

_____

_____

_____

_____

Take time each day to focus on what is going well, no matter how small. It could be your health, a friend or stranger's smile, a safe place to live, your family pet, a book you are reading, or an event you enjoyed attending.

Go out and explore your new home and
neighborhood. What did you find?

_____

_____

_____

_____

_____

_____

_____

_____

_____

_____

_____

_____

_____

_____

_____

_____

_____

_____

_____

_____

_____

_____

_____

_____

_____

_____

_____

_____

_____

_____

_____

_____

_____

_____

_____

_____

_____

_____

"When you're curious, you find lots of interesting things to do." – Walt Disney

What has surprised you about your new home? Your new neighborhood? Your new city?

_____

_____

_____

_____

_____

_____

_____

_____

_____

_____

_____

_____

_____

_____

_____

_____

_____

_____

_____

_____

_____

_____

_____

_____

_____

_____

_____

_____

_____

_____

_____

_____

_____

_____

_____

_____

"When one door of happiness closes, another opens; but often we look so long at the closed door that we do not see the one which has been opened for us." – Helen Keller

What has surprised you about your new school?

_____

_____

_____

_____

_____

_____

_____

_____

_____

_____

_____

_____

_____

_____

_____

_____

_____

_____

_____

_____

_____

_____

_____

_____

_____

_____

_____

_____

_____

_____

_____

_____

_____

_____

_____

_____

"We either make ourselves miserable or we make ourselves strong. The amount of work is the same." – Carlos Castenada

What has been harder than you expected about the move?

_____

_____

_____

_____

_____

_____

_____

_____

_____

_____

_____

_____

_____

_____

_____

_____

_____

_____

_____

_____

_____

_____

_____

_____

_____

_____

_____

_____

_____

_____

_____

_____

_____

_____

_____

_____

_____

_____

_____

_____

_____

_____

"The difference between winning and losing is most often not quitting."
– Walt Disney

What has been easier than you expected about the move?

_____

_____

_____

_____

_____

_____

_____

_____

_____

_____

_____

_____

_____

_____

_____

_____

_____

_____

"The secret of getting ahead is getting started." – Agatha Christie

What are some new places you are looking forward to going?

_____

_____

_____

_____

_____

_____

_____

_____

_____

_____

_____

_____

_____

_____

_____

_____

_____

_____

_____

_____

_____

_____

_____

_____

_____

_____

_____

_____

_____

_____

_____

_____

_____

_____

_____

_____

_____

_____

_____

_____

_____

_____

~ You are stronger than you think! ~

What made you laugh today?

_____

_____

_____

_____

_____

_____

_____

_____

_____

_____

_____

_____

_____

_____

_____

_____

_____

_____

_____

_____

_____

_____

_____

"Every time you find some humor in a difficult situation, you win."
– Avinash Wandre

What can't you truly live without? Try to think of what you need versus what you want . . .

_____

_____

_____

_____

_____

_____

_____

_____

_____

_____

_____

_____

_____

_____

_____

_____

_____

_____

_____

_____

_____

_____

_____

_____

_____

_____

_____

_____

_____

_____

_____

_____

_____

_____

_____

_____

_____

_____

_____

"Most of the problems in life are because of two reasons: we act without thinking or we keep thinking without acting." – Unknown

In 5 years from now, where do you want to be?

_____

_____

_____

_____

_____

_____

_____

_____

_____

_____

_____

_____

_____

_____

_____

_____

_____

_____

_____

_____

_____

_____

_____

_____

_____

_____

_____

_____

_____

_____

_____

_____

_____

_____

_____

_____

_____

_____

_____

_____

_____

"Dreams are necessary to life." – Anais Nin

What are some fun ways you can fill the time as you begin to make friends?

_____

_____

_____

_____

_____

_____

_____

_____

_____

_____

_____

_____

_____

_____

_____

_____

_____

_____

Make the most of your free time: explore your new city or surrounding area, play tourist, join a club or team, or pick up a hobby that you've always wanted to try. Take the initiative to introduce yourself to others, and don't be discouraged, it takes time!

What is your favorite thing so far about your new home or school?

_____

_____

_____

_____

_____

_____

_____

_____

_____

_____

_____

_____

_____

_____

_____

_____

_____

_____

_____

_____

_____

_____

_____

_____

_____

_____

_____

_____

_____

_____

_____

_____

_____

_____

_____

_____

_____

_____

_____

"What screws us up most in life is the picture in our head of how it's supposed to be." – Unknown

3 things that made me happy today:

_____

_____

_____

_____

_____

_____

_____

_____

_____

_____

_____

_____

_____

_____

_____

_____

_____

_____

_____

_____

_____

_____

_____

_____

_____

_____

_____

_____

_____

_____

_____

_____

_____

_____

_____

"If you can't fly then run, if you can't run then walk, if you can't walk then crawl, but whatever you do you have to keep moving forward." – Martin Luther King Jr.

What does it mean to you to 'be yourself'?

_____

_____

_____

_____

_____

_____

_____

_____

_____

_____

_____

_____

_____

_____

_____

_____

_____

_____

_____

"Be yourself; everyone else is already taken." – Oscar Wilde

Do you find it easy to 'be yourself' when making new friends?

_____

_____

_____

_____

_____

_____

_____

_____

_____

_____

_____

_____

_____

_____

_____

_____

_____

_____

_____

_____

_____

_____

_____

_____

_____

_____

_____

_____

_____

_____

_____

_____

_____

_____

_____

_____

"Be who you are and say what you feel, because those who mind don't matter, and those who matter don't mind." – Bernard M. Baruch

Have you been able to find new friends with whom you share common interests? What has been the best way you have found to make friends? What are other things you could try?

_____

_____

_____

_____

_____

_____

_____

_____

_____

_____

_____

_____

_____

_____

_____

_____

_____

_____

_____

_____

_____

_____

_____

_____

_____

_____

_____

_____

_____

_____

_____

_____

_____

_____

_____

_____

_____

_____

"Be not afraid of going slowly, be only afraid of standing still."
– Chinese proverb

What is something new you have tried in the last month?

_____

_____

_____

_____

_____

_____

_____

_____

_____

_____

_____

_____

_____

_____

_____

_____

_____

_____

"You only live once but if you do it right, once is enough" – Mae West

Is there something you should be trying right now
that you are avoiding? What are you waiting for?

_____

_____

_____

_____

_____

_____

_____

_____

_____

_____

_____

_____

_____

_____

_____

_____

_____

_____

_____

_____

_____

_____

_____

_____

_____

_____

_____

_____

_____

_____

_____

_____

_____

_____

_____

_____

_____

_____

_____

"Don't fear failure. Fear being in the exact same place next year as you are today." – Unknown

In what ways have you taken advantage of your new fresh start?

_____

_____

_____

_____

_____

_____

_____

_____

_____

_____

_____

_____

_____

_____

_____

_____

_____

_____

"Isn't it nice to think that tomorrow is a new day with no mistakes in it yet?" – L.M. Montgomery

How have you been at keeping in touch with old friends so far? Have you kept in touch with the people you expected to?

_____

_____

_____

_____

_____

_____

_____

_____

_____

_____

_____

_____

_____

_____

_____

_____

"Do not give up, the beginning is always the hardest." – Kemmy Nola

What don't you like about your life right now? What can you do to change this?

_____

_____

_____

_____

_____

_____

_____

_____

_____

_____

_____

_____

_____

_____

_____

_____

_____

_____

_____

_____

_____

_____

_____

_____

_____

_____

_____

_____

_____

_____

_____

_____

_____

_____

_____

_____

_____

_____

_____

_____

"It has been my philosophy of life that difficulties vanish when faced boldly." – Isaac Asimov

Who or what do you miss the most?

_____

_____

_____

_____

_____

_____

_____

_____

_____

_____

_____

_____

_____

_____

_____

_____

_____

_____

"Sometimes when things are falling apart they may actually be falling into place." – Anonymous

What are you excited about?

_____

_____

_____

_____

_____

_____

_____

_____

_____

_____

_____

_____

_____

_____

_____

_____

_____

_____

_____

_____

_____

_____

_____

"Courage doesn't always roar. Sometimes courage is the quiet voice at the end of the day saying 'I will try again tomorrow.'" – Mary Anne Radmacher

What are you curious about?

_____

_____

_____

_____

_____

_____

_____

_____

_____

_____

_____

_____

_____

_____

_____

_____

_____

_____

_____

_____

_____

_____

"Everybody is a genius. But if you judge a fish by its ability to climb a tree, it will live its whole life believing that it is stupid." – Albert Einstein

Once you have been in your new home for a month or two, reread your past entries and look back on the progress you've made. How are you in a better position now than you were right after the move?

_____

_____

_____

_____

_____

_____

_____

_____

_____

_____

_____

_____

_____

_____

_____

_____

_____

_____

_____

_____

_____

_____

_____

_____

_____

_____

_____

_____

_____

_____

_____

_____

_____

_____

_____

_____

_____

"When everything feels like an uphill struggle, just think of the view from the top." – Unknown

What are you relieved about?

_____

_____

_____

_____

_____

_____

_____

_____

_____

_____

_____

_____

_____

_____

_____

_____

_____

_____

_____

_____

_____

_____

"My entire life can be described in one sentence: it didn't go as planned, and that's ok." – Rachel Wolchin

What are you hopeful about?

_____

_____

_____

_____

_____

_____

_____

_____

_____

_____

_____

_____

_____

_____

_____

_____

_____

_____

_____

"Every time I thought I was being rejected from something good, I was actually being re-directed to something better." – Steve Maraboli

What was your favorite memory from the past week?

_____

_____

_____

_____

_____

_____

_____

_____

_____

_____

_____

_____

_____

_____

_____

_____

_____

_____

_____

_____

_____

_____

_____

_____

_____

_____

_____

_____

_____

_____

_____

_____

_____

_____

_____

_____

_____

"The harder you work, the luckier you get." – Gary Player

What have you learned about yourself through moving?

_____

_____

_____

_____

_____

_____

_____

_____

_____

_____

_____

_____

_____

_____

_____

_____

_____

_____

_____

_____

_____

_____

_____

_____

_____

_____

_____

_____

_____

_____

_____

_____

_____

_____

_____

_____

"No matter who you are, no matter what you did, no matter where you've come from, you can always change, become a better version of yourself."
– Madonna

What advice would you give to others moving with their families?

_____

_____

_____

_____

_____

_____

_____

_____

_____

_____

_____

_____

_____

_____

_____

_____

_____

_____

_____

_____

_____

_____

_____

_____

_____

_____

_____

_____

_____

_____

_____

_____

_____

_____

_____

_____

_____

_____

_____

_____

_____

"When writing the story of your life, don't let anyone else hold the pen."
– Unknown

Three Simple Rules in Life

1. If you do not go after what
you want, you will never have it.

2. If you don't ask, the answer will
always be NO.

3. If you do not step forward,
you'll always be in the same place.

— Unknown

Good luck on your journey!

*(and remember, as you become more comfortable with your
surroundings, don't forget what it felt like to be new and be sure to
reach out and welcome other new students!)*

Other products available from Essential Engagement Services:

The Essential Moving Guide For Families: Practical advice to ease your family's transition and create a sense of belonging

The Essential Moving Guide: Practical advice to quickly create a sense of belonging and settle in

The Essential Moving Guided Journal (For Pre-teens): All About Me, All About My Move

Just Graduated Guided Journal: Preparing For Life After College

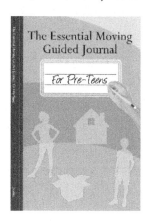

facebook.com/EssentialMovingGuide
twitter.com/MyEsntlGuide
pinterest.com/EssentialGuide/

Made in the USA
Monee, IL
27 April 2022

95494120R00085